Caregiver Burnout 101

A SURVIVAL GUIDE

By

G. G. Geraldino

⚠️ Reader Advisory ⚠️

Brutally blunt and filter-free.

The only things I ever sugar-coat are cookies.

Uncensored.

Contains adult content.

Unsuitable for the ultra-sensitive.

Not intended for the easily offended.

Unanimously unliked by the uptight.

⛔ Warning ⛔

Profane and/or vulgar language

Graphic violence

Sexual explicitness

The Official Legal 💩

Any likeness, semblance, or similarity to any person or persona — whether real, altered, fictional, AI, anime, animated, cartoon, celebrity, character, or public figure — past or present, living or deceased, is completely coincidental and utterly unintentional.

So… sorry.

Not sorry.

Dedication

This is dedicated in honor of my bonus parents. Thank you for loving me and believing in me. Thank you for being the best parents and grandparents ever. I've been called many names in my life, but the very best is being called your daughter.

Acknowledgements

Thank you for your inspiration, Lynette Weldon at Living True. Thank you for encouraging me to start journaling as part of therapy and healing, and for believing in my author journey before I even believed in myself.

Thank you, Diane Warren, for our many years of friendship and shared love of animals. Your songs are truly the playlist of my life.

Thank you to my Sweetie and my babies for your patience, compassion, and support. Thanks to all of my pets for your constant and unconditional love.

Music credit and thanks go to: Sidewalk Prophets, Jelly Roll, Tauren Wells, Citizen Soldier, Phil Wickham, Jason Crabb, Jordan Feliz, Hillsong Worship, Yes, Creed, Kelly Price, Whitesnake, Soul II Soul, Kesha, and Dory from *Finding Nemo*.

Quotes by Rosy Grier and Morgan Freeman.

About the Author

Born and raised in the beautiful Midwest, Ms. Geraldino relocated to Southern California in 1987. She has endured more than enough to have broken many times, yet her motto remains: Keep Getting Up!

Ms. Geraldino has started over—again and again. It is her hope that by sharing her stories, others may gain strength, insight, and perhaps avoid having to learn those lessons in the same way.

In 2003, she founded a successful in-home pet care business. In addition, she devoted herself to human welfare, serving as a caregiver for her elderly parents during hospice and for others who have crossed her path throughout the years.

This book is the first in a series of her tales from the trenches. Now, she's playing by her own rules.

Non-conformist.

Unconventional.

Unwilling to fit any mold.

Introduction

The G~Series

~seven-ish~

Sequentially unfolding storylines — intimately intertwined and intricately interconnected. Based on lots of real-life stuff and tons of real-ly fkt-up $h*t.

I hope to somehow help someone, somewhere, in some way by sharing significant life lessons I had to learn the hard way… so hopefully you won't have to ~too.

Table of Contents

Chapter 1 — When Caregiving Becomes Your Life

Caregiver Burnout!

Yes, it's a real thing!

Disclaimer:

I am not an "expert".

I don't have any special degrees, certificates, or fancy titles.

I have been a Caregiver for most of my life.

Saved/sober 33 years and counting, I am walking the walk -

So can talk the talk.

I hope these stories help bring hope, direction & encouragement in some way.

Spoiler alert: Finding a trustworthy therapist and joining a peer support group really does make a world of difference! Just knowing that you're not all alone in your struggles changes everything! Having a group of others facing the same challenges and offering alternative ideas and solutions is absolutely priceless!

Nothing in life (or death) comes easy. The more you want for something, the harder it is to get.

NOT TO BRAG
BUT I TOTALLY
GOT OUT OF
BED TODAY 👍

Chapter 2 — Raised to Carry the Weight

I've found that there is no such thing as a straight line between point A and point B.

Every time I step onto what appears to be a straight path, I get detoured onto a twisted obstacle course, which is totally overrun by tiny little circus clown cars, and the clowns are dropping their juggling balls all over it!

When I was still a child, I had to take care of my younger brother. I even took his beatings for him from our abusive, narcissistic birth-mother

(But that's another story)

Now, whenever I say Mom-Grandma or Dad-Grandpa, I am referring to the fabulous family who took me in and called me daughter and loved me even in the midst of my brokenness.

(But that's another story too)

Stop stressing out! God knows you are doing your best Trust Him. He will make a way when there seems to be no way.

Chapter 3 — The Day Tomorrow Never Came

I was helping mom with her health issues for years; I went with her to all of her lab tests, doctors, and treatment appointments. I cared for her after her open heart surgery over the years and throughout several spinal surgeries. I helped while she was in the hospital, in the nursing facility, and then finally back at her home. Every day revolved around taking care of her, driving her to doctor appointments, helping with meals, filling her pill box, monitoring her medication schedule, assisting with her nebulizer breathing treatments, as well as taking her on regularly scheduled walks outside to visit the Angel on the corner and help her do physical therapy exercises.

On her very last day here on earth, I was blessed to be able to spend the whole day together with her. First thing in the morning, she came with me to drop my son off at school, then she had an appointment with her primary care physician, after that we went to see her pharmacist to pick up new & refill prescriptions, then we walked to the lab for blood tests. We did get to enjoy a delicious lunch together at Senior Fish, where we shared a super seafood quesadilla with extra sea scallops and sipped on sangrias.

After lunch, I took her to a cardiologist appointment, who did an EKG and an echocardiogram. Grandma learned for the first time that day that her heart wasn't actually heart-shaped.

The doctor said her heart was doing quite well considering that the pig mitral valve replacement surgery was done over 15 years ago. As we were leaving his office, the doctor simply suggested that she add a banana to her diet every day. We were really late getting to the Dojo for my son's MMA practice, but we were luckily able to watch the last ten minutes while he trained for his upcoming Martial Arts Competition. It was a really, really long day; we had been running around for over twelve hours. When we pulled up to her house, I asked Jory to walk his Grandma up the steps to her front door. She stopped at the top of the steps to wave to me. Something urged me to jump out of the car and run up the steps to give Grandma a goodnight hug.

We told each other goodnight and "I love you, I'll see you tomorrow."

Her tomorrow never came.

She died in her bedroom from a heart attack just three hours later, on 9/9/19.

The next morning, Grandpa and I had to meet with the coroner, go to the cemetery, plan her funeral and celebration of life, and deal with insurance companies' forms and legal documents. It all had to be completed at that exact instant.

Tons of crucial decisions had to be made, and Everything had to be paid for in full on the spot.

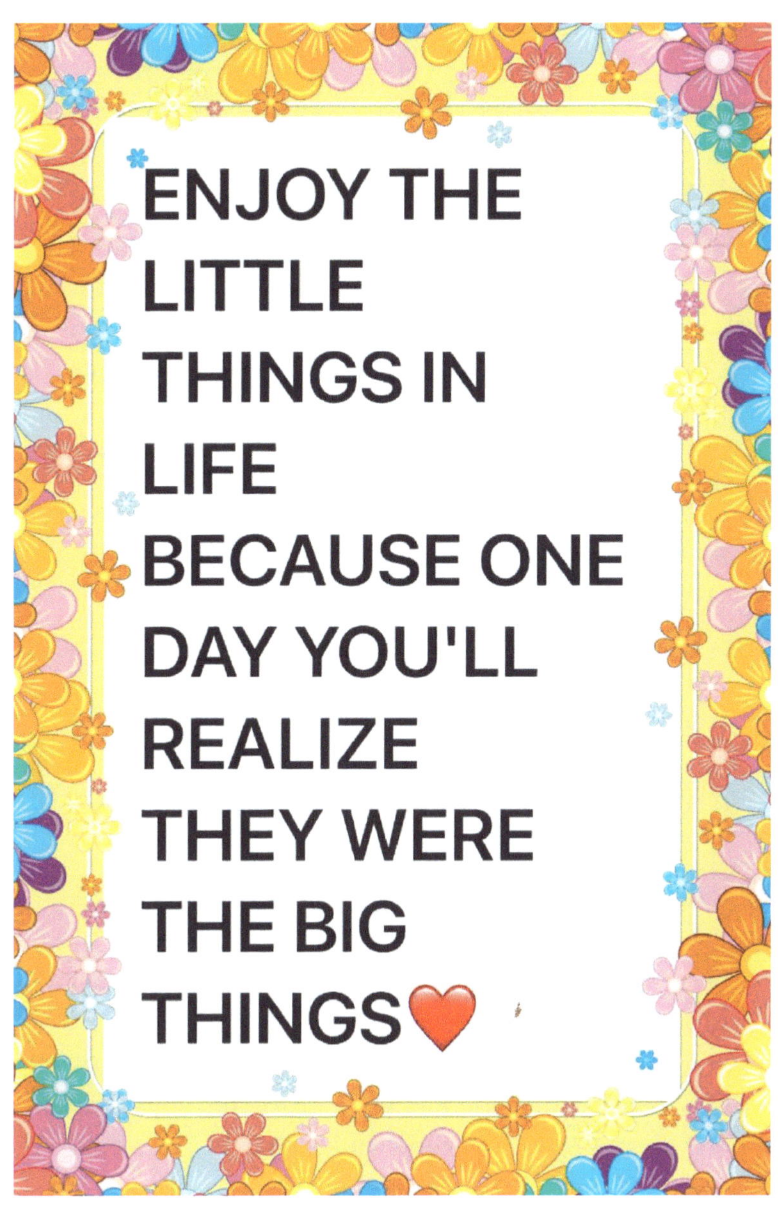
ENJOY THE
LITTLE
THINGS IN
LIFE
BECAUSE ONE
DAY YOU'LL
REALIZE
THEY WERE
THE BIG
THINGS❤️

Chapter 4 — When the World Stopped

A few months later, along came Covid, and it turned the entire world upside down.

My daughter was one of the first to catch it - before we even knew what it was. She was deathly ill for nearly a month; she even missed our family Christmas gathering for the first time in her entire life.

My son started attending school via online Zoom meetings while sitting on the couch wearing his pajamas with either the bird on his head or the cat on his lap. He had to learn quickly, at a fairly young age, how to be independent and totally responsible for himself while I was out working during the day.

I continued to work full-time doing animal caretaking, pet sitting, and vet-tech house calls throughout the entire quarantine.

I became a Face-Mask Fashionista, I literally had a mask to match every outfit!

I have been classified as an 'Essential Worker'. A caregiver's work is essentially endless! People and Pets need continuous care; every living being needs to be fed & loved on, every single day.

I do have to admit, I really enjoyed all the peace and quiet alone with the animals; we all got to share a lot of extra special bonding and cuddle time with no other people around to interrupt us. There were actually some very good things that happened because of the Covid shut down: less crime, less traffic, and fewer auto accidents, no homeless people on the streets, no litter on the sidewalks, wild animals walking around freely and unafraid. There was no Smog in downtown Los Angeles for the first time in, well, basically - Ever! The mountain and coastal views were absolutely breathtaking, no filters needed in any of the spectacular photos I took during the pandemic!

That turned out to be the calm before (or in the middle of?) the storm.

Be the change
you want to
see in the
world-
What you do or
say can make
a difference!

Chapter 5 — A Mother's Heartbreak

In 2021, my daughter Bethany was officially diagnosed with severe chronic endometriosis. The doctors and the nurse practitioners recommended several different courses of action for treatment, but due to multiple ongoing complications and the damage it caused, her fallopian tubes and her left ovary are completely immedicable.

As a result, she most likely will never be able to get pregnant or have a baby naturally. The helplessness and grief over her pain and the loss of a child she would never be able to have was indescribable.

Be the reason someone believes there are still good people in the world.

Chapter 6 — Preparing for Goodbye

Six months later, my dad was diagnosed with multiple forms of late-stage cancer.

Immediately upon his diagnosis, we knew what we needed to do before **The End.**

The morbid preparations were incredibly hard, but they provided Dad with the peace of mind of knowing he got to make the decisions for himself — and that they wouldn't become an additional burden for us to carry in our mourning.

1 — We went to a lawyer to create a will.

2 — Designate me as the power of attorney.

3 — Put the house and assets into a trust.

4 — Go to the bank to convert all funds into the trust account and withdraw emergency cash.

5 — Meet with the priest at church to prearrange the memorial service.

6 — Prepay end-of-life expenses at the funeral home.

7 — Gather and organize all important documents, and file for pension benefits.

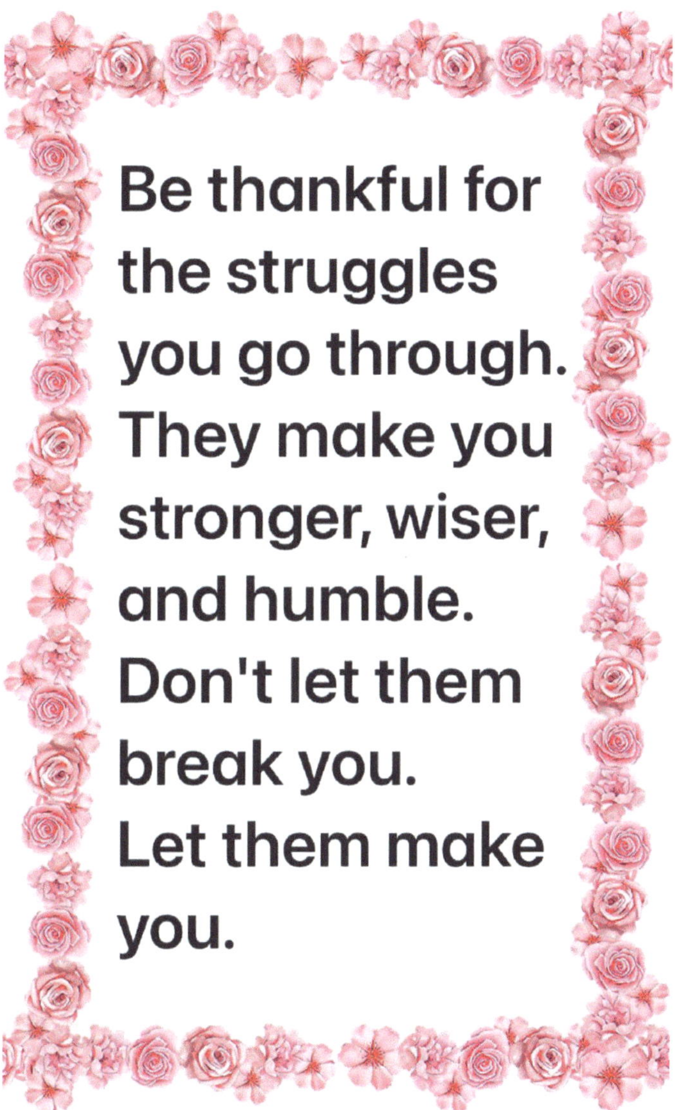
Be thankful for
the struggles
you go through.
They make you
stronger, wiser,
and humble.
Don't let them
break you.
Let them make
you.

Chapter 7 — Living on Empty

I put my life on hold to take him to all of his lab and doctors' appointments, specialists, medical procedures, multiple surgeries, chemotherapy, and radiation treatments. I made sure he took his medicines as directed, as well as ran all of his errands, did his shopping, brought and/or prepared his meals, and handled all of his legal and personal business.

All the while, trying to keep his illness a secret from the whole family, as he requested. Dad was always the rock of the family. He was a stoic example of loyalty, reliability, and responsibility.

Seeing him cry for the first time ever after beginning radiation was just too much to take.

Like a fkn dumb-💩 I started smoking cigarettes again after being smoke-free for nearly a decade.

Many people, especially family members, were really mad at me for missing 'important' events.

No one understood why I couldn't just tweak my schedule. Because they didn't know that it wasn't my schedule.

My dad's health declined rapidly; he was placed on in-home hospice care in August 2023, and was totally bed-bound by December. We learned another lesson the hard way, unfortunately, he hadn't checked the correct box on the disability insurance application form when he originally signed up for Medi-Care 30 some years ago, and so he was deemed ineligible for desperately needed health care services. My daughter and I were his primary caregivers, personal assistants, nurses, chefs, and patient advocates.

A 'normal' day would start at 6 am, I'd pack my son's lunch and take him to school, pick up Dad's La Opinion newspaper, and meet my daughter at her grandpa's house to change his diaper, give him meds, and feed him breakfast. Then out to take care of my morning pet-sitting jobs, then back home to feed my pets, handle phone calls, paperwork, and some computer business, etc.

Follow-up call with the hospice nurse who only came 3 days a week for about 30 minutes to (maybe) change a diaper and feed lunch. By 2:00, I'm driving to my Hollywood job, to take care of my clients' cats and birds, then pick up my son after school or from volleyball practice, take him with me for evening pet sitting jobs, then home to cook dinner, then head back to over to Dads house to medicate, feed dinner and change his diaper before bed.

I'd typically get home somewhere between 1 and 2 am. My eyes barely closed before the alarm was ringing again.

Every single day, every single night, weekdays, weekends, even on holidays;

All the days, weeks, and months just whirred together or disappeared entirely.

Caregiving is a full-time, 24/7 job; it is mostly thankless work, totally overwhelming, and completely exhausting.

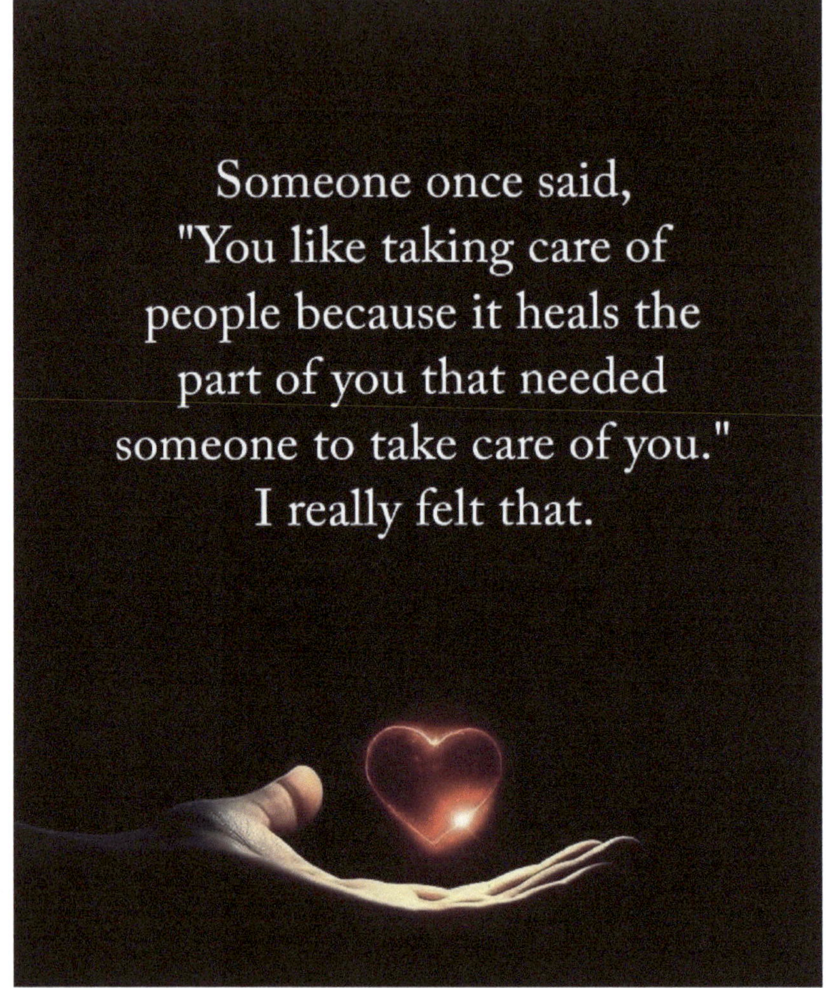

Someone once said,
"You like taking care of
people because it heals the
part of you that needed
someone to take care of you."
I really felt that.

Chapter 8 — The Breaking Point

Through it all, though, it was a labor of love, a true privilege, and a real blessing being able to honor such a remarkable gentleman!

I literally gave away everything I am and all I had in me to care for my family, but I wasn't putting anything back into myself. I was running on empty, entirely on fumes and adrenaline.

Well, the inevitable happened, of course, I "broke down" ☐ Got stuck somewhere in a time loop between April 3rd-5th. I completely lost my 💩 I was crying hysterically and shaking uncontrollably. By sunrise, the tears slowed to a trickle, leaving dry salty streaks down my cheeks and a numb, blank stare, like a deer caught in the headlights, frozen and unable to move. My sweet husband offered to take our son to school that morning so I could try to get some rest.

The phone wouldn't stop ringing, non-stop, long-winded messages left on the machine.

Finally, I called to make an emergency appointment with my psychiatrist asap. I was told that I had to wait 3 days!

Phantom-functioning on autopilot.

Crisis Cruise Control.

On the day of our scheduled appointment The doctor was over 20 minutes late. When he signed into Zoom, he was obviously distracted and clearly uninterested. He actually called me by the wrong name before asking how I was doing.

I started to tell him I thought I had another nervous breakdown, and I was having a really rough time. He cut me off and actually said that he didn't have time to listen to me because he had other Patients waiting.

He told me to try another mood stabilizer and add a prescription sleeping pill. He said he had to go and wanted to schedule my next visit. □

Declined

Dissed and pissed

Disconnect.

Done.

A few hours later, I tried to go out to clear my head. While running some errands, I had a full-blown anxiety or panic attack in my car in the grocery store parking lot. I sat frozen in my car for nearly 2 hours. I realized then that all the Doctors and their drugs couldn't fix me.

Worrying doesn't take away tomorrow's troubles it takes away today's peace.

Chapter 9 — Finding My Way Back to Faith

Something, on that miserable day, made me turn to worship music on the radio. It really seemed to help brighten my mood a bit.

I started working with a marvelous mental health therapist the following Monday. She suggested various relaxation techniques and self-guided meditation. She also recommended that I look into the 'worship music thing' more.

I texted a few friends from my old church the next day to ask where they were going to church now.

Our old church, The Harbor, had closed four years prior, shortly after Covid. Most of the people I spoke with were still church shop-hopping, one has still never even responded … Catnyss Rivers got back to me on 4/11 (with Information). She had been in the water praying over me during my third baptism in 2012.

(But that's another story.)

She invited me to the Church of the Foothills for their Sunday service at 10:00 am. She let me know that a few other former members of The Harbor were going there now as well.

On Friday, I had some unexpected, complicated issues to deal with between the doctors, the hospice company, and the Department of Senior Services.

The day had just about disappeared, and I still needed to get the bird burrito, pick up my son from volleyball practice, and take him with me to do my Hollywood job.

I pulled into the Jack in the Box drive-thru line and saw André, my favorite homeless buddy, who was standing there with his cute little dog TC. I waved them over to my car. I always keep 'extra cash.'

in my car door for those in need. I played with TC and asked André how he was doing.

I was concerned, since I hadn't seen him in a few weeks.

He answered,

"I am blessed."

He asked me how I was doing.

I confessed that I was feeling really worn down and stressed out, and how I was running late… Then he asked me, "Do you know what you need to do?"

"No, André, what do I need to do?"

He said,

"Just pray" 🙏□

I thanked him, said God Bless □, good night, and pulled forward to the pick-up window. I thought about his wise advice and put on my worship playlist for the drive.

On Saturday morning, my daughter's dad helped me hold Grandpa up on his side so I could clean him, change his diaper, and bandage him. I had my music on, and Marius asked what I was listening to. I told him this song is Prodigal by The Sidewalk Prophets,

"Here, listen to this part."

♪♪♪ Wherever you are, whatever you did

It's a page in your book, but it isn't the end

Your Father will meet you with arms open wide

This is where your heart belongs ~ Come running like a prodigal!

He totally loved it! I let him know that I was going to check out a new church on Sunday and said he could come with me if he wanted…

The very instant I stepped in the door at Church of The Foothills, I literally felt like I got hit or something slammed into me, or maybe jumped up from inside of me, I actually stumbled backwards.

When I took another step forward, I saw a sign that said Welcome Home near the chapel door. Inside the chapel, up on the stage, I was amazed to see half of The Harbor's old worship team! I sat in the front pew on the right side. I smiled and waved at my old friends. Marlon, the worship team leader, set his guitar down on the stand, came down off the stage, walked over to my pew, and welcomed me to the church with a big hug! Huge, happy tears started streaming down my face!

Pastor Patrick Soleil started preaching about the Holy Spirit and the need for regular refilling with His word to be refreshed, recharged, and ready for the world. Just like a car won't run without gas, a person cannot run on an empty tank either. You must keep being refilled to be able to give anything away to help others. I had entered the church that morning with nothing left in me. I was empty and completely dried up. I stayed late after service for some extra fellowship. By the time I left, I felt revived, energized, and filled with new hope. I literally felt like I got Born Again, Again!

(But that's another story.)

If you simply can not understand why someone is grieving so much for so long, then consider yourself fortunate that you do not understand.

Joanne Cacciatore

Chapter 10 — When Responsibility Finds You Again

A few days later, my BFF called; her hubby had a stroke and was taken to a nursing care facility. I went to visit.

For years, I've tried to share my testimony with them, but they weren't ready. That day, we spoke a long while about Jesus, salvation, and Heaven. They both got saved. My BFF's hubby passed the next morning while I was taking care of Grandpa. He finally accepted Jesus and got saved, too! Two days later, he passed away in his room,

in his bed, surrounded by loved ones, secure in his salvation, with the peace of knowing he was going to be together again with Mom in Heaven.

He left me with two new titles, Estate Trustee and Landlord, but with no money for any of the bills that had been piling up.

No problem.

It's fine.

I'm fine.

Everything's fine!

I never even got a chance to mourn. I immediately had to deal with life insurance and the bank and the Catholic Church, plan his funeral mass, and celebration of life, place an ad, and then plan to interview applicants for two new tenants so I'd have enough money to pay the mortgage and utilities. (But that's another story.)

To this day, I'm still looking after my ex, Marius, who has basically become like another brother to me. In addition, I am also the primary caretaker and "life coach" for my younger brother, who suffers from Multiple Sclerosis. I rescued him (again) from an abusive and toxic relationship with a narcissist in the nick of time! He barely even made it out of here with his life in July 24. (But that's another story.)

Chapter 11 — Choosing Healing

I started working with a fantastic caregiver therapist and support group, and my hubby and I started couples counseling together.

I joined several other groups, as well, for extra support and inspiration. I knew I needed all the help I could get!

The best investment you can make is in yourself for your own health, well-being, peace, and strength.

If you're anything like the vast majority of the caregivers I have encountered over the years, you are probably wearing multiple hats, juggling three or more jobs at once, and, simultaneously, carrying the weight of the world on your shoulders.

Who do you know would be willing, or even able, to step into your shoes? What do you imagine would happen without you there to fix everything? Would it all fall apart? Maybe.

Caregivers are essential ♥□□

You matter!

Self-care is not selfish; it is an absolute necessity:

It works if you work it, but

It won't if you don't!

What are you going to do for yourself today?

Yesterday is in the past.
Tomorrow isn't
promised.
Today is the present.
A present is a gift to be
treasured.
Don't squander it
looking for what's next.

Chapter 12 — Lessons From the Fire

My Top Takeaways:

1 — Put on your own oxygen mask first before attempting to help others with theirs. You can't do it all — if you're dead.

2 — Do all things in love and kindness.

3 — Treat yourself with the same patience and compassion you would show your child or a loved one.

4 — Remember, no one is perfect! Cut out the negative self-talk.

5 — Celebrate your little victories, because sometimes that's all you get. Focus on the good instead of getting discouraged by the what-ifs, coulda's, woulda's, and shoulda's. Is your glass half empty or half full? Reframe your thinking!

6 — You are someone's role model; practice what you preach. Others will do as you do, not as you say.

7 — Cultivate an attitude of gratitude. There is always something to be thankful for — or a lesson to be learned.

8 — Pray every day. There is nothing too big or too small for God to provide.

9 — It's okay to ask for help — really, it is!

10 — It's alright to cry. Crying takes the sad out of you; it might make you feel better. — Rosy Grier

11 — Adopt a pet. They're the only ones on earth capable of giving pure, unconditional love ❤

12 — Plan ahead. Being proactive is WAY better than being reactive.

13 — Go outside, enjoy the sun, breathe in the fresh air, take a walk… (such a great time to have a dog ☺)

For God so loved the world that He gave us dogs. The love you see in your pup's eyes reflects the love our Heavenly Father feels for us.

BTW — God spelled backwards is Dog □

Dogs are God's way of proving that we were never meant to walk alone.

29

THERE IS NO
DOCTOR NOR
ANY DRUG
BETTER THAN
PUPPY KISSES
ON YOUR
FACE

Chapter 13 — Hope, Strength, and Daily Grace

This touching poem was shared by a friend in my caregiver support group:

Empowered Caregivers at Living True Coaching by *Lynette Weldon*

"Life As a Caregiver"

We mourn the life we thought we'd have.

Grief is never-ending.

Hopes and dreams are put on hold.

Aches in my heart are everlasting.

Our souls are anchored in loyalty.

Though our spirits fade in the wind,

We are the unsung heroes.

Fighting for our lives with no end.

~ By *Racquelb Poetry*

Chapter 14 — Inspirational Quotes and Uplifting Playlist

Here are a few songs, inspirational quotes, and verses that have really helped me in my healing process and for daily motivation:

♪♪♪ I Am Not OK -

by *Jelly Roll*

♪♪♪Famous For -

by *Tauren Wells*

♪♪♪You Are Enough -

by *Citizen Soldier*

♪♪♪Battle Belongs -

by *Phil Wickham*

♪♪♪ Good Morning Mercy -

by *Jason Crabb*

♪♪♪The River -

By *Jordan Feliz*

♪♪♪Broken Vessels -

By *Hillsong Worship*

♪♪♪ Hold On -

By *Yes*

♪♪♪ Higher -

By *Creed*

♪♪♪ It's My Time -

By *Kelly Price*

♪♪♪Here I Go Again -

By *Whitesnake*

♪♪♪Keep On Moving -

By *Soul to Soul*

♪♪♪ Dear Me -

By *Kesha*

♪♪♪Just Keep Swimming -

Sung by *Dory in Finding Nemo*

Matthew 11:28

Jesus said, Come to me, all of you who are weary and heavily burdened, and I will give you rest.

Philippians 4:13

I can do all things through Christ who strengthens me.

John 3:16

God so loved the world that he gave His only Son so that whoever believes in Him will not perish but have eternal life.

Psalms 23:6

Surely Goodness and Mercy shall follow me all the days of my life

(♪♪♪ this verse is actually a song too, I'm singing it right now🎤)

Be sure to visit our website and sign up for the email list to be among the first to hear about upcoming appearances and new book release dates. Visit **https://gggeraldino.com/**

How do we
change the
world?
One random
act of kindness
at a time
- Morgan
Freeman

35

"Share your thoughts in a review and enjoy a discount on my upcoming book."

www.ingramcontent.com/pod-product-compliance
Lightning Source LLC
Chambersburg PA
CBHW040900110726
48005CB00001B/137